D1384838

Flying Mosquitoes

by Janet Piehl

Lerner Publications Company • Minneapolis

For my Madison moving crew—Cailin, Bridget, Barrett, and especially Amanda Moss and Amanda Silha

Lerner Publications Company
A division of Lerner Publishing Group
241 First Avenue North
Minneapolis, MN 55401 U.S.A.

Website address: www.lernerbooks.com

Words in *italic* type are explained in a glossary on page 30.

Library of Congress Cataloging-in-Publication Data

Piehl, Janet.
    Flying mosquitoes / by Janet Piehl.
        p.   cm. — (Pull ahead books)
    ISBN-13: 978-0-8225-5932-0 (lib. bdg. : alk. paper)
    ISBN-10: 0-8225-5932-3 (lib. bdg. : alk. paper)
    1. Mosquitoes—Juvenile literature. I. Title. II. Series.
QL536.P47 2007
595.77'2—dc22   2005024185

Manufactured in the United States of America
1 2 3 4 5 6 — JR — 12 11 10 09 08 07

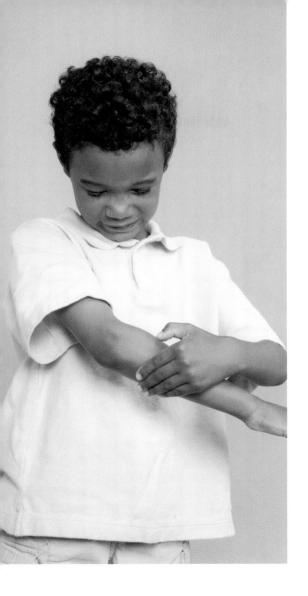

Scratch, scratch.
What is that
itchy bump?

The bump is a mosquito bite.
It was made by a mosquito.

A mosquito is a kind of animal called an *insect*.

Insects have six legs and three main body parts.

Most insects also have wings.
A mosquito has two wings.

A mosquito has two long *antennas* on its head.

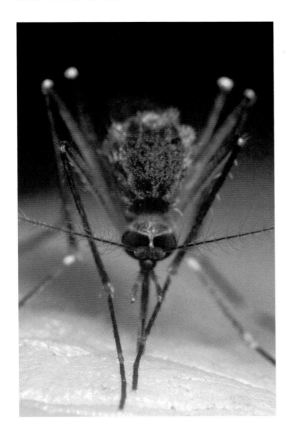

A mosquito hears and smells with its antennas.

It sees with two big eyes.

A mosquito uses its *proboscis*
to bite. A proboscis is like a straw.

A male
mosquito uses
its proboscis
to suck juices
from plants.

Only female mosquitoes suck blood.

Some female mosquitoes suck blood
from people. Others bite animals.

Why does a female mosquito
suck blood?

She sucks blood to get food.
Blood is her meal.

This female mosquito is getting ready to lay eggs. She must suck some blood in order to lay her eggs.

ZZZZ! The female flies off to find food.

She lands on a person's skin. She sticks part of her proboscis through the skin.

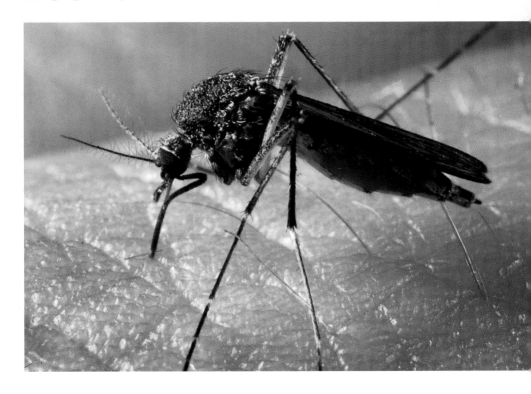

She sips blood through her proboscis.

The female leaves behind some of her *saliva*. The saliva causes an itchy bump to form.

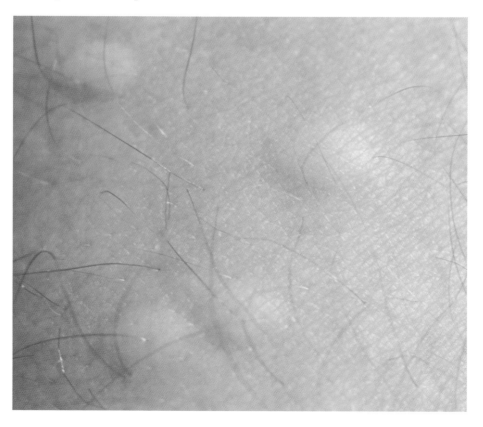

This mosquito is full of blood.

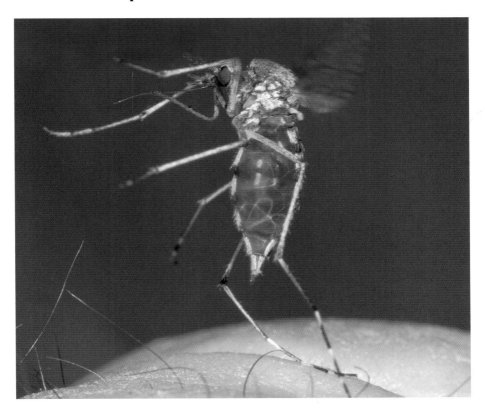

Soon she will be ready to lay
her eggs.

The female flies away to find some water.

Most mosquitoes lay eggs in water, such as swamps, lakes, or puddles.

The mosquito lays her eggs.

Eggs laid by some kinds of
mosquitoes stick together and
float. They form an *egg raft*.

Baby mosquitoes hatch from the eggs after a few days.

Young mosquitoes are called *larvas*.

The larvas swim in the water. They eat tiny things that live in the water.

The larvas grow and grow.

Soon each larva changes into a *pupa*. A thin skin grows around the pupa.

An adult mosquito comes out
of the skin after a few days.

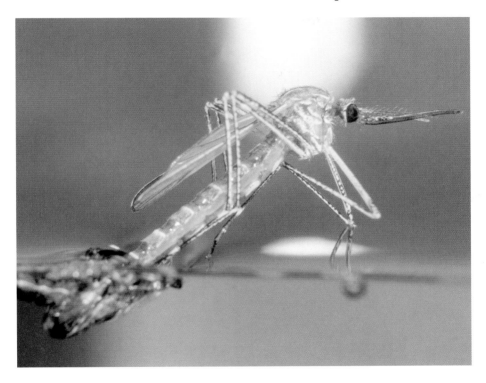

The mosquito leaves the water.
But it does not go far.

Most mosquitoes live near water.
Some live in forests. Do mosquitoes
live near you?

Mosquitoes come out
at night to feed.

But they are
in danger
when their
enemies
are near.

Some insects,
birds, bats,
frogs, and
spiders hunt
and eat
mosquitoes.

People also kill mosquitoes. Have you swatted a mosquito?

ZZZZ! Oh no, here comes a mosquito! Put on your bug spray!

Find your state or province on this map.

Do mosquitoes live near you?

Parts of a Mosquito's Body

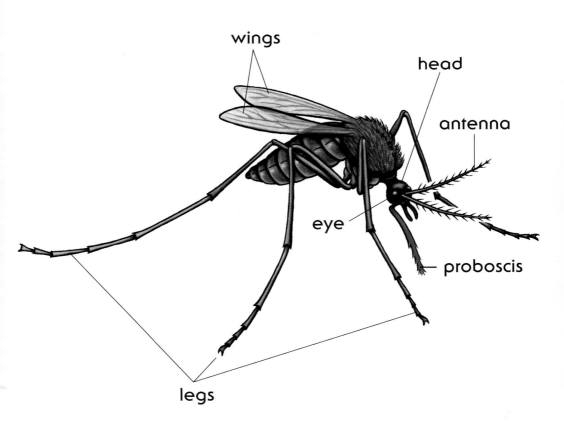

wings

head

antenna

eye

proboscis

legs

Glossary

antennas: long, thin feelers on a mosquito's head that allow it to hear and smell

egg raft: a group of mosquito eggs that stick together and float in water. They look like a raft.

insect: an animal with six legs and three main body parts. Most insects have wings.

larvas: young mosquitoes that have hatched from their eggs

proboscis: the long, hollow part of a mosquito that it uses to suck blood or plant juices

pupa: a young mosquito covered in a thin skin. A mosquito becomes a pupa after it is a larva and before it is an adult.

saliva: liquid from a mosquito's mouth. A mosquito leaves behind saliva when it sucks blood.

Further Reading and Websites

Hey! A Mosquito Bit Me!
kidshealth.org/kid/ill_injure/bugs/mosquito.html

Morgan, Sally. *Flies and Mosquitoes*. North Mankato, MN: Thameside Press, 2001.

Mosquito
http://www.enchantedlearning.com/subjects/insects/mosquito/index.shtml

Siy, Alexandra, and Dennis Kunkel. *Mosquito Bite*. Watertown, MA: Charlesbridge, 2005.

Index

Photo Acknowledgments

The images in this book are used with the permission of: © Dwight R. Kuhn, front cover, pp. 7, 9, 10, 13, 17, 19, 21, 31; © Todd Strand/Independent Picture Service, p. 3; Centers for Disease Control and Prevention Public Health Image Library (CDC)/William Brogdon, p. 4; CDC/James D. Gathany, pp. 5, 8, 20, 27; © Michael Durham/Visuals Unlimited, p. 6; © Carl R. Sams II/Peter Arnold, Inc., p. 11; CDC/Dr. William Collins, p. 12; © Johan Lind, p. 14; © John Kohout/Root Resources, p. 15; © R. F. Ashley/Visuals Unlimited, p. 16; © Rob Fienhage, p. 18; © age fotostock/SuperStock, pp. 22, 23; © Dr. Martin Dohrn/Photo Researchers, Inc., p. 24; © Lowell Georgia/CORBIS, p. 25; © Bill Beatty, p. 26. Illustrations on pp. 28, 29 by Laura Westlund, © Lerner Publications Company.